The Way She Told Her Story

Diane Jarvenpa

Poems

The Way She Told Her Story

Poems by

Diane Jarvenpa

n
RIVERS
e
PRESS
w
MSUM

Cover and interior design by Christen Nagel
Author photo by Nick Lethert

The publication of *The Way She Told Her Story* is made possible by the generous support of Minnesota State University Moorhead, the Dawson Family Endowment, and other contributors to New Rivers Press.

This activity is funded in part by a grant from the Lake Region Arts Council through a Minnesota State Legislative Appropriation.

For copyright permission, please contact Frederick T. Courtwright at 570-839-7477 or permdude@eclipse.net.

New Rivers Press is a nonprofit literary press associated with Minnesota State University Moorhead.

Nayt Rundquist, Managing Editor
Kevin Carollo, Editor, MVP Poetry Coordinator
Travis Dolence, Director
George McCormack, MVP Prose Coordinator
Thomas Anstadt, Co-Art Director
Trista Conzemius, Co-Art Director
Thom Tammaro, Poetry Editor
Alan Davis, Editor Emeritus

Publishing Interns:
Laura Grimm, Anna Landsverk, Mikaila Norman, Laura Grimm, Anna Landsverk, Mikaila Norman, Lauren Phillips, Cameron Schulz, Rachael Wing

The Way She Told Her Story book team:
Turner Blaufuss, Travis Dolence, Alexa Gerber, Hailey Wilmer

 Printed in the USA on acid-free, archival-grade paper.

The Way She Told Her Story is distributed nationally by Small Press Distribution.

 New Rivers Press
c/o MSUM
1104 7th Ave S
Moorhead, MN 56563
www.newriverspress.com

For Aili, Hilja, Kristiina,
Elisabet, Anna, Cecilia,
and all the women in my
family who came before me.

Contents

IV

V

Summer is twice beautiful—
Leaf on tree and grass on ground
But I shall soon be a third—
  I a leaf waving
  I a flower heard of
  I a sweet stalk swaying

—The Kanteletar

I

I Was a Quiet Child

Olin kukka ollessani,
kasvaessani kanerva,
vesa nuori noustessani.

I was born a mud-puppy,
sun-headed, bare feet wed to bog,
bell flowers and inky caps for pillows,
aspen leaves and blown weeds soft as bed.
All spells lay in rushes,
their thousand taproots singing.
Only soft beats of blue moth wings,
only footfalls of shy one
tracking birds.

I sat with reindeer,
slept with moose,
the cold hub of earth
polished by ice and sun dogs.
My thin tree self
brittle in wind,
my fingers tipped with stars.

They wanted me
to walk away.

But this is where you seek it,
thunder raven, bee-eater sky,
tireless track of beetle,
air stirred up by owl,
jewelweed thumbed by rain.

This is where each hair
you own knows when
to walk the predawn fog,
swim inside the cool night loop
of glimmerfish, listen
to trees unfurl stories

of mortals and their fates
all tied up and then
beautifully undone again.

This is where
I crouch with voles,
roost with nightjars
as constellations open
blue asters all around,
admit truth is eloquent
as any duck, any map
its migrant wings pursue.

Polaris hung an answer
for a shape-shift girl,
in a forest lost for wanting,
and I cut a sort of path
and walked a kind of hunger
as I ate the morning sun
and the lilies filled my bones.

As a girl I was a flower
twig of heather, young green sapling
berry of the arctic bramble
they whispered to me
golden one.

Watching My Daughter

She balances like a piece of sky,
  her dress flared in blue kingfisher wings,

training her feet as they measure fence,
  certainty of belief called out.

These are my slim hours
  to study all that headlong passage,

noisy in its details,
  strong in its physical hungers,

her many crows of knowledge
  a calculus of measured flight.

A blur of particulars
  packed into each day,

gleanings of honeysuckle, river of potions,
  a mother's newly hatched pain, observing

footprints of imagination turning
    and walking away.

The Sky Drops Rooms of Snow

Here it is again,
the demand
to reinvent and devise
plentitude from a cold ground,
a bargain of lost pleasure
in each still life
caught in ice.

It is easy to fall,
copper-tint chill water
runs in the veins,
slighting of brittle sleet
glazes over reed and rock.

There it is though,
making its speech like marble pebbles
tossed from Greek statues,
neglected nouns on drifts,
speedy frown and muscle slap of wind,
each syllable a skate blade
sent out to set a covert trail.

But each deliverance
of polar sky,
parabola of frost
on my window
alters the cast,
begs an aubade against
giving up
before it clouds
all we know.

Because after all,
is it not winter
and even in the midst
of every bright, cold bit,
do we not spark?

Wash Day

There is a clear labor
in sudsing something clean,
the all-liquid watchful strokes,

an accumulated path of past and future.
A mindful disappearance
in the dipped-soft tongues of cloth

beneath a warm blue sky.
Iron to cloth
as you straighten, kiss the edges

in quiet acceptance
of the day and all the common acts
that rescue us,

hands that sew a button,
bird sitting on an egg,
lips that spell

new words on babies—
all that mad devotion
to begin again.

The Rune Singer

She fills her birch-bark shoes
with leaves
for the deep snow,

skims sour milk
with an alder spoon,
axes logs for the sauna

and sits in the back of the barn
to sing
of the green-throated forest.

Renders eggs into oceans,
wine from stones,
the sun and moon into witches' hay,

women singing themselves into fish,
into a quick power
no one wants to see in them.

She returns alone
to the dark kitchen
and boils her onions,

unfolds mended sheets,
uncoils
her long silver braid,

and sleeps a different breath of notes
until another dawn
is strewn with magpies,

cows lost again
in the rye field, coffee
over-bubbling on the fire.

She chants the sounds
and motions of the White Sea,
honey from the grasses,

arctic berries that turn
into moon-haired girls,
the constant failings

and invented pleasures
of men and women,
as she casts out

her incantations
of this cold, mysterious world,
ringing like a copper bell.

A Generous Fever

Ostrabothnia, Finland 1708

See here on the side of this barn?
That is my name, Annikka.
My family lived over there past
the rye field, beside the endless pine,
on the hill looking down at the lake.
There were many girls in the house,
but I was the only one
who dug up red worms
with my crochet hook.
The other girls kept quiet,
sewed their flaxen shirts,
all got married, had fat, pink babies.
We never saw them again.

I got married too,
they made me almost pretty
with starflowers in my hair.
He went to school
and then it started,
they didn't like his new words in Greek.
They had a trial, but he died of the Fever.
Another fever swept across the western hills,
witches were in every pile of hay,
every other church pew.

One day they told me I was guilty,
old lady Aina got a bellyache.
She heard me singing on that same Sunday
outside her window.
I could tell them it was my mother's favorite song,
but she would be a witch.
I could say my father was walking with me,
he would be a witch.
I could say old lady Aina

11

always had a bellyache,
ate too much fish fat and pancakes.

But they looked inside my pockets.
Dragonflies.
I had found them down by the lake.
But they said I had killed them.
I had sung a spell.
They put my ankles into the stocks
on two different Sundays.
One for each dead bug.
After that I took to my long walks
far over hills, the lake a tiny mica chip,
the village a distant piece of grit.

And this is the way I learned to do it,
picked baneberry and stitchwort,
kicked fireflies off the folds of my skirts,
emptied my pockets of dust and bee wings,
threw them on a chanting fire.
And what never was
attached itself,
alive as any muse,
any shrewd, dark animal
breathing in the shadows.

Leave the Farmhouse

Go, walk away
from the clutter of spoons,
the white birch chairs that stammer
across the pine floor.

Leave behind the purpose of the sink
with all its cleanings and cold rapids.
Let your bare feet walk out into the chickweed,
let the only purpose of your legs be
that they carry you onward

past that story, the old man
you never married
who crashed fences with his drunken head,
wiped the sweat off his horse
with one hundred dollar bills.

Follow your children
who boarded over windows with sullen nails,
to walk over sea, sky, cloud,
dropping old ghosts like dead flies,
dipping into the future like a hot new cure.

Use the map on the back of your hands,
pitch your losses like broken pebbles into the wet sky,
warn us of the distant world of every youth,
how strong that yearning to ignore and repeat it all,
your blood song growing inside us
like the circles you make in the river
with each stone's throw.

Apart

Tampere, Finland 1915

Dear Daughter,

There is a sparrow here
that sits in the lilac
gathering purple fragrance in its wings,
maybe there is a small brown bird
in your morning that sings its sacrament to the day.

There is November filling the air
with its sweet dying dust,
maybe where you are
there are birch trees holding fast
to their lemon leaves.

There are pinecones that have fallen
in a storm, their construction
of tongues a puzzle in the palm.
Do you hold one up to the sun like this,
searching for an answer?

There is blue sky here with those
thin sewn clouds you might find
on a linen robe
with a moon like a cut pearl.
Do you see this same moon now,
count days until it rims round?

Daughter, you and I,
no matter how many
seas or countries
come between us,
still have tree, sky,
have moon and bird,
an inheritance
of common things.

The sun moves over
all roofs and grasses,
do we not
dream together here,
under this single star?

II

Skylark on a Stone

She leaves the boarding house each day
under gun-metal skies to walk basalt and lava flow,
wet wings of the lake folding
over her immigrant configuration.

In the forest her camouflage soul
wavers and obscures,
sparrows sit on her lap opening seeds,
fox runs right over her shoes.

She fell right in with those teams of circling skirts,
shipboard and nestled too close,
loss and dream packed tight inside their carpet bags,
the wet leaves of all those shawls

soaking up damp and recent failure.
Her clothes are now shiny in spots,
the sharp angles of her body confounding stitches,
there is a vagrancy in not belonging,

she fumbles her new name like a fallen button.
This land is not what she read in the letters,
her feet trip uncut paths, empty hands
hold invisible maps with unwritten grids.

Still she is training her young heart
to modest settlings,
slurry of yeast in a blue bowl,
resurrection of black ink inside a book.

When she looks into the forest
she thinks she sees her mother,
arms heaped with lupines
on Midsummer's Eve.

She goes back down to the lake
where each cold wave
slowly wipes away the old geography,
the helpless telling of her distant story,

her bones becoming light, learning
how to lean in, accept
this new weight
in this new wind.

When She Filled the Bowl

We were brought together
in the middle of that dense map of trees,
where galaxies of mosquitoes spun around your ears,
chinks of sunlight squeezed through pine needles.
There was a woodbine confusion
on all the paths at night.
If you didn't follow the buzz and gasp of stars,
you could be lost for good.
I lay in my bed alone, raw wind
scouring away every silence.
I dreamed a deep green sea,
men sloshing up on shore,
pulling their seaweed beards,
holding empty plates.

I couldn't believe the money.
When you haven't got any and it is given,
it seems you are walking inside golden halos,
all words spoken are soft and round,
hunger becomes a distant corner of dust
far from anything in your life.
But not really that far.

The lumber camp mess hall smelled of sweat
and bread dough, the famished forever
digging in their bowls.
Great mounds of men appeared and disappeared
all through the day, their large slabs of hands waited in turn,
before the river of milk, pancakes stacked like cordwood,
scooping oatmeal to their chapped boy lips,
soups and stews to ride the dark cold nothing of their bellies.

I learned how to sandwich mercy and power
between thick slices of bread
and when every scar of your life
pulses with failing,
sugar and butter shine brighter
than any old-world sun.
I was the only woman in
this home of axemen.
Nobody bothered me,
the future was already written,
money was the only word of love.

Secrets Live in Small Rooms

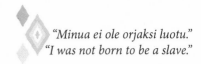

"Minua ei ole orjaksi luotu."
"I was not born to be a slave."

Perhaps this morning
will be different,

but she knows it is the same
as always. There is her immigrant past

that finds its level every day,
sometimes storm, sometimes shock,

sometimes as distant as a story in a thin newspaper
where you nod your head in faint recognition.

There is her work, which in simple truth
is boiling, scrubbing, folding people's lives

into clean, sharp corners that poke at others
who are soft or have sharper corners still.

It is work for those with what is called wealth,
who like to wallpaper their lives

with a shimmering indifference.
It is in a home where *receive*

is the common language of the day
and the elegant interlocking

of need and want cross-stitch endless demands.
This is the place where she has learned fatigue

can be a pure kind of grieving.
Sometimes when the pigeons

start their wing-scrapes at her window
and the whole smoky city is still asleep,

she sits up in her little maid bed,
studies the four corners of her room

she has lived in many years
tucked down the hall from those she serves,

and invents for herself
a different future.

A private life,
a home with her children,

digging in her own garden,
stirring spoons in her own pots,

speaking of dreams
with her forbidden husband

that involve her own heart
each and every day of the week,

instead of only on her one day off.

The Way She Told Her Story

She told them she was leaving
for New York City.
But your children . . . they said.
Yes, she said, I know I have children,
and she got on the train.

Men have children too,
plenty of men were seated on the train.
She had learned how to cross the earth
and become someone else,
but she knew the land circles back
and then who do you become?

She had been like a stone,
thrown across continents,
still she liked the train's voice,
its score of wheels on switchbacks,
the open window's half-hum
fingering her hair.

What she liked best was how a voice
could shape words,
how those words sat on her tongue and came out
firecrackers, sharp and hot
tossed from the stage
to the dark shapes seated below.

Everything was an old story
and everybody always wanted to hear another,
be it doves or ash, the world lit with candlepower.
Here is where she found a kind of home
with velvet curtains and floors to sweep,
a pile of scripts thick with ink
and social observation,
artists muscling wit and props.

Only here she could
fashion a tale,
take this stone and toss it out there herself
and make it light and loose
as a field of stars,
passed from mouth to air,
radiant, before it disappeared.

By Hand

She tastes it in her sleep,
field of rye flowers
set into crumb,
cloud of butter seeping.

Torching a lantern,
she coaxes the climate,
dips knuckles into potato water,
begs bubbles in the starter,
ballad of milk,
sour slag of rye.

She dusts air with salvos
as flour refutes old gripes,
the laying on of small hands,
rhythm of gathering,
the proof.

Each envoy of new beginning
bargains for lapsed hunger,
melancholy stirred in and out of the fire.
The scholar and the broken-hearted,
the drunk and the bright young maiden
sit around her groaning board.

Cutting of crust,
sliced up myth,
tang of truth
on the tongue,
Eucharist with buttermilk.

Because this bread
questions no one,
leavens expectation,
champions everyone,
fixes even this sad, flat horizon
with praise.

The Round World Has Its Work

First she makes them clean.
Brings them to the dim-lit room,
warm from large black stones.

Gives them mint,
spits out herbs, casts out bad spirits—
black stars, broken shadows.
Push-pull of steam
softens the air as each hour expands

and contracts with the body,
centering on that one simple thing,
pucker of the navel,
and the round moon drawing on
its internal sea.

For a week they might sit
together in the dark,
just like her mother did
rocking and rubbing women
round and aching.

They stay warm in half-light,
soup boiling over flame,
listening to the belly
and all the old stories
in its changeling bulge,

its hunkering urge to obey
and divulge its mortal shape,
matching breaths and cries
to sparrow and wind

before sticky hairs, almond-shut eyes
feel the dip and fall of the ladle,
before they bring the child,
fragrant as birch,

out to the house filled with kitchen fires,
out to the raw, empty arms of the father—
the new mother all wing and suckle,
salt angel to new flesh.

She slowly walks away
over the path of milkweed,
her bent body aching,
rubbing her blue-veined hands.

She picks clover and sips its sugar
as she sits down
in the purple meadow,
face to sky,

thinking this is where
she would banish herself for good,
breathing in deep
the sun-struck world.

Fine Art in the Boardinghouse

Imagine many strange people in your home,
scouring sleepy flesh in your tub,
forever denting your puckered mattress,
forking runny yellow of egg,
mooring dusty boots down hallways,
desperate wish to un-attach from the day,
work that never washes off.

You are in charge of all
shadow shapes that sit at the table.
Make the whole a canvas,
pull sea from the clay pitcher,
quarter moon from the rind of cheese,
luster that fades, luster that magnifies
white flowers in a bowl.

Split the curtain so
to reveal that soft line of the wooden rake
leaning in the budding orchard,
fit old lace, best knotted
over scarred table, secured with copper pot,
basket strewn with linen holding lemons.
Frame it all with the carved beauty of quiet,
answer to noisy order of chaos.

If their prayers match up
with too much melancholy,
move the sun yourself
through the open window.
Fix your firm, bright arts
amid the ache, shift and blur
of day to week to year.
Remember why it matters,
that exact color,
that single slant of light.

The Reader

I tucked books into my apron pocket,
my sister said, "Baggage of another tongue."
Mother tongues braid into blood forever,
this was another way the world split open.

While stirring soup, pounding bread,
wringing boiled linens,
hidden chapters beckoned,
itched to enter each task of hands.

Domestic fuss turned sour,
the stamped black spheres,
hypnotic spindrift, brokered for my time.
Who wouldn't want this small sea

on which to float,
trade a shallow pool of gray dishwater
for a fast-cut sail in ragged wind?
Soon it was routine migration,

entering paragraphs
to cry there at the edge
of some distant turf,
sing in that precise, defined light.

And each time I returned to matching utensils,
driving needles around the darning ball,
the loose spots in the lace of my former self
had filled in with a fluency

and a weight,
stunned by the open page,
eclipse of the closed book,
that subtle inner shift,
the likewise slender logic of hope.

New Tongue

The town here looked just born,
maybe it was how the houses
rose from dirt,

sidewalk boards plugged with shiny brads,
no trees, only dust from the sawmill
in my hair, and that way the road just ended.

I was a girl a long way from home,
I knew how to find my way around in forest dark,
but here the sun set its vast vernacular,

continental night.
This was a new century,
everyone carried a raw itch of hope,

all night labor brought new plans,
acceptance of reinvention,
journeys were common as salt.

What was left to do
but remove boots,
turn up the kerosene

over storm and muscle of new words.
Twisted twine of verbs and distillate nouns
asked for someone else to speak them.

I chewed each hardened syllable,
softened predicates in my china cup.
Prehensile modifiers coiled

and hung like loose birch skins.
My speech warped and wound around
in serious illusion for weeks,

I worshipped the passive,
its silver line, soft and distant,
adjectives seemed fleet of wit, hard to coax.

Soon the tiny spoon I dipped into the lyric jar
became a ladle into the stew
and I was well-fed.

I never married. I wasn't any good
at leaning into those geometrics, matched
ironed sheets or scrubbed corners.

Instead I taught kids who walked
with tight fists and questions,
who breathed no words of this country.

Their curious immigrant pens
piled up stories
with deep-colored dialect,

spelled out riddles,
whispered histories,
ghost-songs of our silent pilgrimage.

Kitchen Science

As thin as a dollar
As many as will lie on a point of a knife
As much as seems necessary

Size of a large plum
Size of a large apple
Half an eggshell full

Dissolve in lump of butter size of walnut
Wrap in layers and layers
of dampened brown paper
Bruise with wooden spoon

Bake in a moderately cool oven
Boil like mad
Cool it (almost)

Ready when hissing hot
Let them scald until a sprig from the broom
can be run through them

Very nice when made right
Will answer quite well

Must be cooked
neither too long
nor too quickly.

Add rich milk and globs of butter—
although fish heads are rich enough.

III

She Slept in Her Own Green Tangle

Each week Emma opened up
her front door and walked past
the co-op where her husband the butcher
cut up meat in any amount you asked.
She walked past the hall
where certain Saturday nights the communist speaker
went so long that some who had come to dance
went home to drink instead.

She found her scrabble of woods,
sat on a fallen aspen,
and opened her field book
to rows of edibles and apothecaries.
There she could find all those clean methods
of order, rank, and phylum that broke down
life into slots, rows, and boxes,
a comforting knowledge
in the certain and the fixed,
not the imbalance of the uncertain,
unpredictable rage,
being hit by a man.

She did know things that burst
from the earth
could be unruly,
burrs and thorns,
itchy oils, rank effluvium,
but the same earth delivered
radials, bells, tubes, and sprays,
flowers born in the axils of leaves,
flowers worn in her buttonhole.

In the wildwood,
the merits of Marx versus Engels
didn't compare to the cattail,
its Cossack asparagus not untasty,
its blown fruit a good stuffing for pillows,
and bittersweet, what a fitting name,
so winning with its delicate orange berries in the snow
but could kill a full-grown horse,
strangulate a forest of trees.

What she found
was a place not unlike her own world
with hidden powers and hungers,
but also that hole in a line of trees
where she walked alone,
blistered and closed off, hidden like a turtle,
sleeping with the wren
and the wheel of the spider,
transcribing with her bloodroot flower
the thousand mercies of the thicket.

Boiling Pot in Embarrass, Minnesota

Peel the potatoes,
skins in single coils,

nautilus of discards,
playthings for the baby.

Whittle wax off rutabaga,
dice into small tricks of love.

Target onion rings with knifepoint,
frugal woman's best friend,

flavor in, sorrow out.
Break off celery stalk,

pale green crunch soon to sponge.
Wedge carrots crisscross,

working down to fractions.
Sliver, skive, and split

to make it all multiply.
Shrug salt from shaker.

Boil. And done.
Feed your family

on one more winter day
where snow covers

most of the windows.
Sit on your chair

against the wall alone,
away from the table,

and watch them.
On each face

a bloom of color
as they spoon the soup,

your heart a single hymn.
When they are done,

bend down to kiss the baby
as he kisses his own hands.

Wash the empty pot
and see how the sun finally appears

at the kitchen window,
track its habit of changing light

across all your daily habits and changes.
Bring your own cool bowl

to your lips
and drink.

Woods Boy

The flu epidemic appeared soft and slow
like a cool wind in woods,
jingling aspen, rippling creek water
and ended in a flattening blast.
My son wakes up one day to sing me
good morning and then that night goodbye.
What does a three-year-old know of death
other than the stepped-on beetle,
the mice drowned in the water bucket,
the cut-up flanks of skinned deer?
He will have the misfortune of being too young
of too many. He will be cast about
like a loose pebble
to my parents reciting bible verses,
cousins' homes filled with barn cats,
and food that has no color.
What he will really grow to know are rivers,
the blurry shimmer of fish,
limbs of trees that break out for sky,
that hold him high like some fallen star.
It is in the woods, in the mist and drizzle,
in that downward curve of earth,
a disappearance and a navigation take place.
Birds with their yearly migrations
will pass over new patches of soil
turned in the graveyards, passing over humans
going through all their motions of loss.
And a young boy watching them fly off
over his only home,
a cold bowl of forest
with totems of pine, glacial silts,
shatters of stones and ruptures of green,
learning how things break apart,
yet somehow keep their weight,
learning how his sorrow is not so special.

Grandmother's Recipe

She and her husband were not convinced of the spirit
that joined us all while sitting in a hard wooden pew,
but there was the warm, yeasty haven
of her communist kitchen, sweet
with fat brown bread and thin pancakes.
She knew lovers liked to dip shared spoons
into raspberry jam and children were forever
concocting winter, their knuckles all snowy
from her piles of flour and pots of sugar.
She knew what she believed, maybe it was Lenin
staring at her from the dining room wall, or the way
berries lured her and the bears to the forest bush,
or that birds had it right, put your back to the past, and fly.
She knew hands held dreams for the belly.
Here she said, this is what you do:
Knead flour, egg and butter, add sugar, fold and knead again.
Fold dough over gently like layers of baby blankets,
fold gently like all those letters I sent to my mother
pretending we were happy.
Roll out, press, stretch and cut fast.
Dot each center flower with a jam, not too sweet,
make it prune, that fruit black as kaamos—*winter dark.*
Then fold into stars and brush them shiny with egg. Bake.
Set them on the Christmas table.
Go ahead. Eat a star. Right now, this is our only heaven.
Sweet and crunchy and bitter in the center.

Mother Ink

For Helmi Mattson

I take the black heap
nothing of letters,
blend story and map,
reflect worry and shadow,
align words into linear columns
cast off from hot metal tattoos.
Pulled from the weight of dream
and despair, I am given speech
from the lips and tongues of others
and make a kind of imperfect song.
And I am an imperfect mother
that sets a table where the underclass
of the world claim their chairs
and tell their stories.
There is always a code and an index
strewn through my day
and the need to edit proliferates.
I could say I ask for nothing
but some kind of truth,
a common language
that answers the watchfulness
and hunger in all of our voices.
But instead I rely on
a linear metamorphosis,
kindled story
to winding sheets,
a wild twist of fortitude
slamming like fists
onto crisp folds of printed pulp.

Lime Island

For singer Katri Lammi,
exiled to mine on Lime Island, Russian Karelia.

I admit I have held
many broken pieces of my life

and had to go on.
I'm not alone in this.

I have sung simply to connect
what is lovely,

what should be,
to explain no one is immune.

Did you feel
the damp this morning?

I wore a scarf today,
for it might rain.

Will the rain hurt
when it touches us?

I think it will feel like a horse's mane,
wild rose petals, sugar on the tongue.

I remember
the warm necessity that love affects.

Can it multiply
an orchestra of migrants

and their delicate stringed hearts,
past the dismissal of all logic,

motion without movement?
"Maybe I got it all wrong"

is a haunting statement
and hollow in its extreme

of bullets hitting skulls.
I hear voices, lake lapping on shore,

women taking care of women,
children in the stables.

There is nothing I can do
after the fact,

but know there is the fact
of a stubborn spring.

I know there are birds in the bushes,
even though from here, I cannot see them.

There is a Song I Climb Into

For Viola Turpeinen,
the first female accordion star of America

It is a dance,
pell-mell gunshot
pogo-stick polka,
too-many beers, never-fear-
your-dreams schottische,
a what-fate-allows tango.

It is a lake,
all swell and skiff of holy rain,
drink for impossible thirst,
a scuttle of flowers
swimming at my ears,
the dark purple deep
suck of mud.

It is a coin on a train track,
the distant groan of freight,
downbeat of wheels,
bright face in the sun,
small clink under cars,
the judged transfer,
that lost story.

It is an old idea,
the unused language of home,
the lost merit in forgetting,
shadow tracery of absence,
salty rind of a distant coast,
birds murmuring through blue air:
listen.

How Laments Build a Meadow

After he died,
I lived in the sauna-cabin by the lake,
my bed a single frame box,
still too big,
linens trailing the thin lace
I made with my mother.
His hands had always circled
over my body beside
those perfect knots
in the constant dark.
I had them bring the body to the sauna
wrapped in those white sheets,
to make him clean
in a slow, warm silence.

One day, I let Ella's sick cow
sleep in the big house.
No one in there, made no difference.
She was cold,
I brought her a blanket.
She slept in the kitchen,
she liked the window there.
I gave her some herbs
and she felt better.
That made them all talk,
boiling tea for a cow.
They loved to talk.
They used to talk about my hair,
it wasn't Presbyterian hair,
more like hay scorched in a devil's fire.
My big hands chopped wood too easy,
my man boots were too loud,
my pipe smoke smelled of dirt.

Then they talked about my speech,
my long laments in the evening.
My sorrow had no English words,
it's no one's business how deep or long
a sadness comes to stay.
They thought I was crazy,
locked me up in the state hospital
with my wild dark hair,
my pockets full of herbs
and unknown words.

I was a strawberry on a hill
A cowberry flower on a hillock
When I sat, the lands rejoiced
When I stood, the walls glimmered
When I danced, the heavens seethed
*When I walked, the tree roots writhed.**

And so I became *the singer*
walking down the wooden corridors
with my bag of bone buttons
jingling,
my voice a bright flower,
my voice a box of tears,
my voice a path of secrets
in this new country forest.

*From the Kanteletar
a collection of ancient Finnish runes sung primarily by women.

By Heat and Flame

For Maija Grotell, mother of American ceramics

Bottle, bowl,
     vase, jar,
          plate, jug,

sit with backbones
straight from the ground,

slick minerals spun soft.
The kiln, a sketchpad until the curve,

relief pattern, the rim-song is right,
seeking those layers like a cracked pearl.

Spiral skin, fine-grained slips worked into
infinity, whirls and drifts of earth conspired.

Chemistry and dream from heft and hands,
fifty pounds of wedged clay

thrown to the kickwheel.
Firing rosebud and melon into pigment—

turquoise, reduced red, plum, flesh pink,
glazes that dig sun from shadow,

flush sea and sky,
breathe in under-waves.

The urgent turn of spherical center,
language of form fixed,

she rises alone, divides, shapes and delivers
a whole—the horizon and the apple,

constellations
and the moon

and all the light
that they contain.

Need for Sweet

Sugar spilled
from mother's hands to hers,
poured vanilla smooth from her vowels.

Sugar pulled fat
through threads of sorrow,
telling lies she wants to hear.

Sugar blended over
her lost tongue,
solace of sweet under sweet.

Sugar in the dance,
shy shoes
standing by the wall,

witness to the wedding,
drifts of glitter,
clear-cut grains of love.

Sugar in the blood, flesh on flesh,
damp heat rising,
taste of clover on wind-pricked skin.

Sugar inside pages of books,
soil jammed with seeds,
clean sheets struck by sun.

Sugar in those many prayers of bees,
that hidden history,
a mother's lyric in the belly.

Sugar-tinge of children's kisses,
their winter-summer
likewise saving grace.

Sugar, begged for in silent mourning,
her jar of tears
tucked behind the pine tree.

Sugar, her common sense muse,
stirred into
a highball glass.

Sugar, dusted across impossible days,
bottled into syrup and slipped
into the corners of any absence.

Sugar, all glue, solvent, effect,
her recurrent dream
of surrender.

Vagabond Girl Has Yet to Marry

The right question got lost,
thin coin down a gutter grate.
I'm not much for logic,
and nagging slows the dance.

I'm all for bridges
that tempt my forest-drunk soul.
I twirl red skirts
right over the vagrant river.

Some days I believe one chooses, or else
I just impersonate a woman who cares.
Melt my heart down to its core
and I might say yes.

Vagabond Girl Sings a Song

Lyrics scrubbed in a cold heaven,
rhymes carved in a rose-moss field,
melody round as plums.

It's an old story
and it whirs in longing,
and it makes mama cry.

It has a bird,
the long rolling of waves,
and quite a bit of sorrow.

I sing it big and kind of ugly,
I sing it small as a hummingbird egg,
I sing it black currant dark with pricks of stars.

Each time I sing it,
wintergreen blooms in my belly.

Vagabond Girl Moves On

Fact is, I see heaven on the perpendicular
from my boots and indirect roads.
All that appeals to girls who stay
in fluffs of dust powder and curtains
is desire in a shuttered box.

The untroubled arms of trees
are a better host to a fever caught alone.
I'm a firekeeper and winds cross over,
riffle flame.

Go ahead, try to tame a hawk;
there's more than wing and talon,
and always a bit of blood.

IV

Crabapple

Every spring she would climb up
inside its white oblivion
lost in a web of bee and flower,
and it was like those poems
where golden ducks carry away the heart
like a lost boat at sea,
her refuge, a garden in the sky,
her hair studded with sticks and petals.

But she was not a maiden from an ancient rune,
she was the single girl who sat in the tree reading
thick books her mother and father read
because she thought they would give her a map,
help her understand what made adults grow silent.
But she did not understand,
though it did make her come back
to those words that spill page to wind.

In the fall she would fill a bucket
so she could eat the sour fruit.
Seizing the hard red ones,
she would bite them
until they made her cry.
Still, she was not really sad,
just annoyed at how
too many sweet things turned sour,
wondering how a friendship
with the sun could have gone so bad.

Dear Karl,

I dutifully read my Communist Manifesto
and neatly wrote out responses for my father
about multiplicity and the abolishment of eternal truths

until I received the nod
and could run outside into the clear blue day,
sneak into the barn and read my hidden stash

of movie magazines about Carole Lombard.
I snuck backstage many Saturday nights
at the Finn Hall while the communist speaker

lectured on the epidemics of over-production
and I watched the band tune up,
slick their hair back, and toss the kids candy.

I sang songs from my little red songbook
that for the rest of my life could make me cry.
This was not invented pain,

this was proof that hunger and neglect
were a shared sorrow that lived inside people's voices.
But we would once again have to just settle

for drinking tar-black coffee
and dancing to the band with the slicked-back hair.
I later married a man who was a file clerk

at the Justice Department, who found the names
of many of those same singing voices
tucked inside Hoover's little black drawers.

But I continued to sing to myself
when I taught in inner-city schools
where teachers were randomly thrown

down the stairs by angry youth,
who could blame them?
And during the collected suburban amnesia

that blanketed my neighborhood with distance and denial,
I tucked hundreds of folded slips into my vanity,
small prayers of pity and fever.

I never could pull off the faithful daughter,
floundered at the happy housewife.
A failed Christian, a failed communist,

I did as you suggested,
I disdained to conceal my views and aims
and did all that was really left for me to do.
I became a poet.

Water Was Her Dream Religion

She steps in and out of her boat,
numbering over all the fish,

all the miles of river
and lake she's crossed,

kneels at the rim of blue,
a sort of forest nun.

Damp wicks of horsetails
and sweet rockets her church candles,

hymns lost in reeds.
She feels rain as threads for sewing,

a dress spilled from green air,
design and pattern pinned

to gravity and gust. Cold, blue,
auroral rapid bubble,

a damselfly praying her way
across skim of phosphorous chill.

Her only way to measure time,
all that heaven floating.

Before She Knew What It Was

For my mother

She decided to look for herself
now that she had some time
and she would actually show up
at a small town park or she would find herself
listening to a song that purged old fears.
Suddenly she seemed to connect to a whole
of something long lost,
an elaborate knot of former trials and errors
now made into a new pattern.
And when she felt her former self meet up
with her present, it wasn't necessarily unpleasant,
more like a swig of something bitter
with the slight relief of salt.
It wasn't about aging, though it was past desire.
It was about doubt honed down by miles.
Did she forget what it was she believed
when she was young? Or maybe she hadn't,
but it had become more of a sour question.
When she was in a car and an egret flew over,
she wanted to pull over now and watch
like it was some sort of message the sky had unspooled.
Or she would cry when she looked at a lake
all mackerel from fog and sun. A lake written by Tu Fu,
painted by Berthe Morisot.
This was not how she was raised,
but now she needed to look at that bird, that lake water,
for if she didn't she had now found a new way to suffer,
because this was a different precinct she was roaming.
For she had found that person
that she had somehow shoved aside,
staring with child eyes.
And she whispered—
Oh yes . . . you. No, don't go too far,
there's more here. More.

View from Here

Turku, Finland

On a rainy day, a man
with a shiny black accordion
played to his family and friends
in the back of a café as I ordered some soup.
They seemed the only happy people in the place,
their music and laughter a kind of staccato
of eruption, the way birds distract the quiet forest,
reminding the solemn stand of pine
they are also there to hold warm eggs and wet babies
and the endless industry of song.
And yes, those gypsies sang,
I had no idea what they were singing,
but they sang like they were building a bridge
out of coins and bells and bolts of silk
and then threw the coins into the river.
They sang, it seemed, because you have to
or you'll get flattened by a world absent of song.
And I ate my soup in silence
with all the others in the front of the café,
but there was a shift. My commonplace spoon
stirred lament and doubt
and a little bit of rapture
all while the accordion player in that back room
sang from a deep place
like a ravine filled with epic loss
as he stared straight past us and out the window.
But maybe he sang, "Look out there you fools,
look at what you are missing!"
But if that is what he sang,
I knew none of us would turn,
we were shy with clouds for eyes.
But if we did turn, I thought
we would see more than the light rain
pearling the windows.

66

Maybe we would see past the slick street
to the tops of the aspen,
over the green grid of the park,
above the city set in its cubist canvas,
checkerboard crops of oats and rye,
cumulus thinning to cirrus—
the sun.

New Widow

She listens to the rain,
rivers down sidewalks,
cool air welcomed like any gift

tied with lightning, ink-black sky
now turned back to cobalt.
She picked hailstones,

spiky and large as urchins,
to place on her aching joints.
All day the town cloaked in cloud,

a hill carved from foggy quartz,
hazy as the women in the nursing home
sleeping in their chairs, their silent heads

wild milkweed drowsy from thirst.
Knots of work and loss
insinuate their way

behind her eyes,
fading scent
of wet gravel and day lilies

move with her sheets as she turns them down.
They always came here after a storm,
now she climbs in bed alone,

listening to the earth drink fast
its promise
of repeating thunder.

She Resists the Fade Away

> *"The more you love a memory the stronger and stranger it becomes."*
> —*Vladimir Nabokov*

It's an easy climb to the roof
to lie down on a mattress
and look up at the sky.
They say moths see color in pale moonlight,
I see sun-struck rock and on its map
those plains we once thought were seas
and those rilles, dry valleys that start
and then just stop abruptly
like a series of thoughts
inside any tired mind.
The moon is moving away from us
over an inch a year.
I lift my hand and it is gone behind my palm.
Gravity bends light,
but we don't understand the distortion.
Old men and women are tucked into cubicles,
their previous lives improbable.
It is all a slow fade
like paintings now out of rotation,
propped in a cool museum basement,
all pigment flake and canvas warp,
secrets in the shadows we can't make out.

Bench by the Hardware Store

Each week I sit on this bench,
scarf tied under my chin, bag of sweet things
from the bakery in my lap, and I tell my stories.

Sometimes I fear I say listen to me
in that way old women do
when no one wants to hear.

If you sit by a river you can hear
how the swiftness of things can be hard to understand.
My life has told me this over and over

and now I am the Rip Van Winkle of the dragonfly,
the hundred sparrows singing songs
in the trees of the gas station.

Some day you too will find light absent
as it fades faster than you thought possible,
and the impatience you carry in your pocket at the ready

will be layered over with unimaginable years,
some holy bruised, some lost, and some quite radiant.
But who wants to hear about the thinning of days,

it makes the breath stop to look up and think past stars
to the black universe that spreads out and out.
I am old and still I look up,

you are young and looking down,
pushing buttons on a lit screen.
What an enormous distance

a small square piece of glass creates
on one town bench.
I wonder, which is closer, you or the nebulae

brewing in the sky?
I once knew a beekeeper
who said he didn't mind the smoke and stings

and nobody to talk to,
because there was always the honey.
I guess we can't solve everything,

but it is easy to make our days lonely.
And where does that leave us?
I am too old to understand your work,

you are too young to hear me talk about
how today I asked yet another young man,
eyes glossed with screen light, his name.
But he never answered.

At the Mosquito Inn

It sits in the middle of a bog,
a forest of pine going on for miles at its back.
Inside, Grain Belt signs and pool tables,
the cloudy glasses of a long bar.

We women sell sugar bread by the restroom,
tell stories we've smuggled in our palms
in a language that whispers strange and bright,
laughter borrowed from our mothers' kitchens,
a union of collective memory,
indifferent to the many ways the body fails.

And we sit before the band
and sing a hundred years of cold grief,
absence, distance, dance.
Songs carried here by our parents
emptied into our pockets to sit blind and dumb
like all silent songs until one is coaxed into air.

We sing of rivers, war, lark, cuckoo,
deep wood desperation,
we sing long and drunk with August beer.
We shape our lyrics in a smoky old century bar
in a town once believed the Land of Hope,
a place filled with dreamers,
red stars tattooed on our thighs.

Mystery and truce are woven
into the invisible bloodlines we inhabit
as we sing the world swift and light,
the room a wooden bowl we spin and stir,
scattering birds and forgotten lies.

Survival Kit

If I was asked to say right here,
right now, what I would like today,
I would stop short, not used to such questions.
Soul frost with ice splinters have gathered
in long stalactite layers.
So to begin with I would say . . . tea.
I would like tea and bread.
A day with sun.
A modest pile of books.
A chair to sink into and not be afraid.
Slow the fierce horse of pain and pick up
something with strings that sounds a lunar note.
Link loss to a new map that legends
contradictions. And these contradictions
would be acknowledged for their unique character
and mystery, the same way we walk
through those national parks
thinking them beautiful,
though large at times, holding many hidden trails.
I would set loose shame,
though it can be a tricky business.
It's not really like lifting a cage latch and letting
bird feet push off from an open pair of hands,
but I've heard it feels that focused, that fragile.
I would name suffering and fold it into origami.
Some days I would rather use my hands
for making paper herons,
the fugue of those ever tinier triangles,
small sharp wounds into small sharp blooms.
Take the broken pieces of this world
and fit them into a new algebra of green hills with trees.
Finally, tell my story in the only way I can tell it,
leaving the afterword for another day.

Mother/Daughter

For Kristiina, Hilja, Aili, and Lilia

It is a shifting place,
not a country,
more a continent with moving borders.
But growth is common

as pencil marks on a door frame.
And height charts push
the heart of the one
holding the pencil.

How to measure this?
It is sitting under a willow—
thin whips of reeds,
pale, slim tendrils of curls,

stretched into glossed leaves
that dress the grass,
drink you in shades of awe.
You observe her

like she was
a monsoon, a moon,
a reckoning of all
the directions in your life

come to an improbable center.
There is more here than the rosy spell of a child,
there is the power of the young
and what is not yet visible

as this small person
puts her shoulder
to what she wants,
unlocks drawers,

arranges maps,
holds a new forever
in the cups of her hands,
sees many angles like Pythagoras

or God.
And you learning again
the disappointment and generous nature
in the arts of memory.

Re-Search

The librarian wheels out a cart
with research boxes six and seven.
I lift off covers with my mother's name.
Drafts and galleys, and also letters I wrote,
folded by twenty-year-old fingers.

Here is an alphabet of a girl,
refusing dark burdens of umlauts,
Nordic plumage of guilt,
collecting new-world jazz,
searchlights for her muse.

Mother's answers, a spoon
at a morning table,
knowing how the word works.
Prepare, season, and eat,
filling tender, vacant spaces.

Weird how our half-rhymes
come together
as if what we were both sorry for
needed a layering of paper
inside a fitted box,
so when curious hands
shuffled the deck,
a ninety-three-million-mile light
found a new story.

There is a circle
and a purpose,
mother and daughter
tucked into this island,
roaming the pages,
speaking our lines,
softer than doves.

What This Immigrant History Research is Lacking

What is underneath.
Spinal cord, bone marrow, skin, scent.
—*Arja Tiainen*

Voice—flutey, braided words in a sirocco,
a velleity bird speaking in spruce trees.
Or more splinters of nails piercing the heart of the matter,
maybe salty as a sister sitting at a bar,
rustling skirts, heels clicking, jabber jaw.
Distinctions of consonants wedged inside a ballad.
Water slapping a washtub, water against raft poles,
light rain on a housecoat.

The lonesome dream of sailing blind
and navigating a new captivity.
Finding a rocky hollow
where the house is built,
dovetailed vocabularies
in a pool of cold wind.

Scent—lamp oil, cucumber, dill,
green wool, green copper, wintergreen,
cold sweat, beer, fish stew, lye,
sour milk, sour bread, sweet pantry dust,
cloudbursts, sauna smoke, mineral springs,
snow falling, trees falling, falling
into a field of violets.

The ice-pitted tunes of old roads,
messages in drawers never found,
tender migrations
of human and bird,
cloud and fear,
lost inside this faint ink
on these thin papers.

Genealogy

The last time I went to Finland,
I brought my daughter.
We drove up and down green hills,
stopped at empty fields
that waved bear grass, hummed
with hill-bottom bees.
We stood at fence lines and stared
at many vacant plots of land
where an ancestor had maybe milked a cow, spun some linen,
meaning and connection not yet assigned.
Sometimes there was a house and a person
who came out to show me a picture of my great-uncle
who died alone of yellow fever. Someone else told me a story
about the arrogant rich guy who drank and gambled,
lost all his property and wound up in a tiny shack.
That would be my great-grandfather,
or *the asshole* as we liked to call him now.
Probably never married my great-grandmother,
the only true link the romantic gift
of his drunken echo lost inside a sorrow cloud.
And what about those three kids who left the country for good?
All I ever got out of them about the homeland
were snake spells and hunger moons.
Did these people matter?
My daughter definitely thought they did not.
It was summer, what was better
than sitting in a car with three adults
who ignored you while they discussed dead people?
Sad, dead people.
And it was painful, for the living ones in the car
were kind of sad too.
The narration of my family story
seemed to lack an arc that contained any sun,
many sentences missed nouns and verbs.

I had a mad need for a message
that teased just out of reach.
But that is how I left them,
a lost arrangement of bones
and unreadable signatures,
set apart at a perpetual distance,
ash and riddles.
I turned to my daughter,
who I kept discovering was awfully good
at paying homage to what pleased her.
There she was looking upward
and smiling at a hundred blackbirds
released into the brisk, wind-blown day.

Grandma Smokes Her Pipe

Inside a bird cherry tree I found
a gibbous moon and hung its pearly eye,
to help me see your round peach face.

You'll soon learn, life is a twisted rope,
weather it soft and supple, make it a swing,
walk it like it's summer sun.

Plant some turnips for your sweetheart,
honey soil will come,
no ghosts will haunt your children.

Don't forget in the center of the heart
is a lie and a truth,
be wary of which sings best.

May lily, wonder violet,
stone bramble, creeping lady's tresses.
Kiss this earth, she's a lonely beauty.

Something You Will Need

For my daughter

A map.
Yours. Use it.
Only you can know
how the roads will turn,
switch back, climb.
Only you can read its latitudes,
trace your finger along the relief route,
steer your way on blue highways.
Go ahead, study those junctions,
rotate directionally
sun/moon, mountain/sea,
plot your course
along mineral brooks,
witch hazel woods.
Devise your own whistle stops,
track your own epicenter,
thumbtack only the towns that matter.
Take your monk's pen
and draw an illumination of cypress or peacocks.
You might keep aware of scale and curvature,
but only if continental drift is involved.
Just remember your projection
will not need to be conventional.
Line up the quadrants
to meet up with the sweet and spice folds,
to find the finest donuts, hottest salsa.
Use as rain shield, Ouija board,
paperback of fables, periodic vector
of wanderings and intentions,
humble candle of transit,
talisman of bearings.
Destination,
a voluminous theory
that keeps expanding,

an artful goal.
If you need to circle back,
fortify, mend,
I will draw this dot
here by the center rib,
the world before the journey,
carried safe in the soft, dark cloth
of your pocket.

Notes

"The Rune Singer"—Rune singers were ordinary women and men who sang the Kalevala and the Kanteletar—epic poetic stories, poems, and chants of Finland, recited in song form. These stories and songs were passed down orally from one generation to the next before Finnish was a written language. Runes were presented in a variety of ways including: to express the state of mind of the singers and their experiences, at festivities that celebrated the life cycle and the coming of the seasons, and charm runes that depicted ancient Finnish life.

"A Generous Fever"—Found written on the side of a barn on the land of one of my ancestors in western Finland—"Emäntänä Annikka Matintytär, joka käräjillä v. 1708 tuomittiin noitumisesta kahdeksi sunnuntaiksi jalkapuuhun." "*Landlady Annikka Matintytär, accused of bewitching was sentenced by the church court in 1708 to sit for two Sundays in foot/ankle stocks.*" Jalkapuu or ankle stocks were a punishment of shame that the church used at this time. If someone committed an act that was considered against the church's morals, the person was locked in jalkapuu in front of the church. Every church had jalkapuu. If the church thought someone was a witch, particularly a woman, sometimes the punishment commanded she be burned alive.

"Mother Ink"—Helmi Mattson was born in 1890 in Finland and moved to the U.S. in 1911. She was an activist in Finnish–American society. A writer and commentator, Mattson was the editor of the leftist women's newspaper *Toveritar* for ten years, and wrote for the newspaper *Eteenpäin*. She also wrote 500 poems, published five novels, and serialized seven other works of fiction in addition to writing full-length plays.

"Lime Island"—Katri Lammi was born in Finland in 1901. She immigrated to the U.S. in 1920. She made her way to New York and married fellow singer and actor Jukka Lammi. They were often seen in main roles at the Workers Hall in New York. The Lammis were among those Finnish-Americans who went to Petroskoi, Russian-Karelia in 1931. "Karelian fever" was the recruitment of members of North American Finnish communities to go to the Karelian region of the Soviet Union to help build a society to implement their ideals.

Recruitment took place in the period 1931–1934, lured by the promise of jobs and better lives, only to meet tragic ends. Between 1931 and 1936 the Lammis continued acting and singing. Political opinions often shifted during the time of Stalin's rule. Her husband was targeted for not singing enough Russian or Karelian songs. He was arrested in 1938 and shot. Katri was also arrested, but her sentence was expulsion to Lime Island in Lake Onega, Karelia.

"There is a Song I Climb Into"—Viola Turpeinen was probably the first woman accordionist to record, and certainly the first female accordion star in America. A second-generation Finnish-American, starting in the 1920s she played the Finnish dance circuit in the Upper Midwest. Eventually she was based out of New York and toured widely. It became a tradition for dancers to see her headlining travelling shows every summer all across the country.

"How Laments Build a Meadow"—The Kanteletar was published in Helsinki in 1840. This collection of more than 660 lyrics and ballads is the companion work to the national epic the Kalevala. And its main source is feminine lyrical song focusing on the female experience. These women's songs dealt with loneliness, community, work, leisure, hate, and love.

"By Heat and Flame"—Maija Grotell was born in 1899 in Helsinki. She emigrated to New York in 1927 and studied at the New York State College of Ceramics at Alfred University. She took a position as head of the ceramics department at the Cranbrook Academy of Art in Michigan where one of her colleagues was the architect Eliel Saarinen. Grotell was considered to be an innovative and gifted teacher, and was known for her experiments in glaze technology. She won a number of awards during her career, and her works are represented in the permanent collections of many museums including The Art Institute of Chicago and The Museum of Modern Art–NYC.

Acknowledgments

Thank you to the following people who helped me with seeking and researching the stories of several of the women who appear in the manuscript and supported my efforts in finishing this book: Risto Kauppi, Eeva Pasanen, Juha Niemilä, Gerry Henkel, Rauno and Ritva Ketonen, Taina Ketonen, Mari Ketonen, Alan Jarvenpa, Robert Jarvenpa and Liz Lofgren. I am indebted to the writings of Varpu Lindström, Marianne Wargelin, and Mayme Sevander. Also thank you to the generous friends who shared the stories of their families, mothers, and grandmothers. And most importantly, I am grateful for the writings of my mother, Aili Jarvenpa. Her poems, essays, anthologies, and papers directed and inspired me to begin the journey into the voices and words of Finnish immigrant women and their descendants.

I also want to extend my gratitude to the team at New Rivers Press who worked so hard editing and making this beautiful book. It is an honor to be one of so many poets, including my mother, that have been published by New Rivers Press. Kiitos.

Eratta

Thank you to the Minnesota State Arts Board for the Artist
Initiative Grant that allowed me to travel Minnesota and Finland
and afforded me the time to work on this book.

Thank you also to Finlandia Foundation for awarding a grant to use
some of these poems and produce the film project *The Way She Told
Her Story*.

These poems appeared in the following:

It Starts With Hope- Center For Victims of Torture anthology Nodin
Press: "Survival Kit"

Knot Magazine: "Bench by the Hardware Store," "Before She Knew
What It Was," "Vagabond Girl has Yet to Marry," "Vagabond Girl
Sings a Song," "Vagabond Girl Moves On"

New World Finn: "At The Mosquito Inn," "Boiling Pot in Embarrass,
Minnesota," "Genealogy," "Mother Ink," "The Rune Singer," and
"There is A Song I Climb Into"

Turtle Quarterly: "Grandmother's Recipe"

Water~Stone: "How Laments Build A Meadow"

About the Author

Diane Jarvenpa is the author of *Divining the Landscape* (New Rivers Press), *Ancient Wonders, the Modern World* and *swift, bright, drift* (Red Dragonfly Press), and *The Tender Wild Things* (New Rivers Press), which received the Midwest Independent Publishers Association book award in poetry. She has received artist initiative and fellowship grants in writing and music from the Minnesota State Arts Board. She is a teaching artist with the Alzheimer's Poetry Project-MN. She is also a singer-songwriter who records under the name Diane Jarvi.

www.dianejarvi.com

About New Rivers Press

New Rivers Press emerged from a drafty Massachusetts barn in winter 1968. Intent on publishing work by new and emerging poets, founder C.W. "Bill" Truesdale labored for weeks over an old Chandler & Price letterpress to publish three hundred fifty copies of Margaret Randall's collection *So Many Rooms Has a House but One Roof.*

About four hundred titles later, New Rivers, a nonprofit and now learning press, based since 2001 at Minnesota State Univerity Moorhead, has remained true to Bill's goal of publishing the best new literature—poetry and prose—from new, emerging, and established writers.

As a learning press, New Rivers guides student editors, designers, writers, and filmmakers through the various processes involved in selecting, editing, designing, publishing, and distributing literary books. In working, learning, and interning with New Rivers Press, students gain integral real-world knowledge that they bring with them into the publishing workforce at positions with publishers across the country, or to begin their own small presses and literary magazines.

New Rivers Press authors range in age from twenty to eighty-nine. They include a silversmith, a carpenter, a geneticist, a monk, a tree-trimmer, and a rock musician. They hail from cities such as Christchurch, Honolulu, New Orleans, New York City, Northfield (Minnesota), and Prague.

Charles Baxter, one of the first authors with New Rivers calls the press "the hidden backbone of the American literary tradition." Continuing this tradition, in 1981 New Rivers began to sponsor the Minnesota Voices Project (now called Many Voices Project) competition. It is one of the oldest literary competitions in the United States, bringing recognition and attention to emerging writers. Other New Rivers publications include the American Fiction Series, the American Poetry Series, New Rivers Abroad, and the Electronic Book Series.

Please visit our website: *newriverspress.com* for more information.